COLOUR IN
SCIENCE

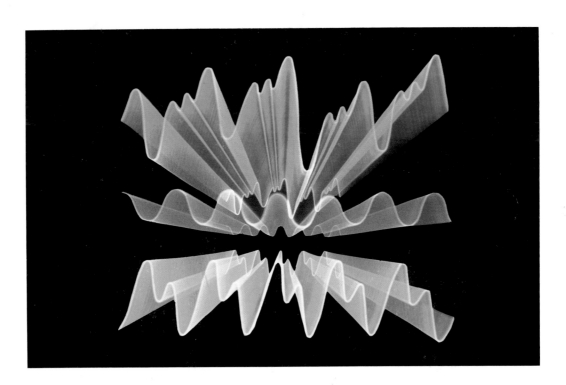

SALLY AND ADRIAN MORGAN

Evans

Evans Brothers Limited

Published by Evans Brothers Limited
2A Portman Mansions
Chiltern Street
London W1M 1LE

First published in 1993

Printed in

ISBN 0 237 51273 4

Acknowledgments

Editorial: Catherine Chambers and Jean Coppendale
Design: Monica Chia
Illustrations: Virginia Gray
Production: Jenny Mulvanny

For permission to reproduce copyright material the author
and publishers gratefully acknowledge the following:
Cover: Main photograph – Fireworks over the Clifton
Suspension Bridge, Bristol – Andrew Plumptre, Oxford
Scientific Films; inset photograph – Coloured light
interference patterns on a variety of petri dishes – Dr
Jeremy Burgess, Science Photo Library
Title page: Computer graphic image of light waves – Fred
Burrell, Science Photo Library
Contents page: Satellite image of the world at night. The
white areas correspond to city lights, indicating the
urbanisation from region to region. The yellow areas
correspond to natural gas flares associated with oil fields,
while the red areas indicate agricultural burnings
Page 6 – (top) MPL Fegden, Bruce Coleman Limited, (right)
David Parker, Science Photo Library, (above) Brown,
Ecoscene; page 7 – (top) Peter Aprahamian, Science Photo
Library, (left) Leaper, Ecoscene; page 8 – (above) Martin
Dohrn, Science Photo Library, (left) Hawkes, Ecoscene;
page 9 – (top) Farmar, Ecoscene, (left above) Hank Morgan,
Science Photo Library, (above) Towse, Ecoscene; page 10 –
(right) Magrath Photography, Science Photo Library, (above)
Peter A Hinchliffe, Bruce Coleman Limited; page 11 – (top)
S Nelson, Bruce Coleman Limited, (bottom) Towse,
Ecoscene; page 12 – (top) Hans Wendler, The Imagebank,
(bottom) David Parker, Science Photo Library; page 14 –
Mary Evans Picture Library; page 15 – (top) Sally Morgan,
Ecoscene, (above) Heather Angel; page 16 – Earth Satellite
Corporation, Science Photo Library; page 17 – (top and
inset) Cooper, Ecoscene, (bottom) Hans Reinhard, Bruce
Coleman Limited; page 18 – (right) Alfred Pasieka, Bruce
Coleman Limited, (below) Geoff Williams and Howard
Metcalf, Science Photo Library; page 19 – (left) Dr Jeremy
Burgess, Science Photo Library, (inset) Alberto Incrocci, The
Imagebank; page 20 – Heather Angel; page 21 – NASA,
Science Photo Library; page 22 – (top) Thomas Buchholz,
Bruce Coleman Limited, (bottom) Michael Freeman, Robert
Harding Picture Library; page 23 – Sally Morgan, Ecoscene;
page 24 – Sally Morgan, Ecoscene; page 25 – Wilkinson,
Ecoscene; page 26 – Hawkes, Ecoscene; page 27 – Sally
Morgan, Ecoscene; page 28 – (top) Towse, Ecoscene,
(bottom) Heather Angel; page 29 – Heather Angel; page 30
– Brown Ecoscene; page 31 – (top) Peter Aprahamian,
Science Photo Library, (bottom) Sally Morgan, Ecoscene;
page 32 – Alexander Tsairas, Science Photo Library; page 33
– Alfred Pasieka, Bruce Coleman Limited; page 34 – (above)
Philippe Plailly, Science Photo Library, (left) Philippe Plailly,
Science Photo Library, (below) Paul Shambroom, Science
Photo Library; page 35 – Bill Longcore, Science Photo
Library; page 36 – Adrian Morgan, Ecoscene; page 38 –
London Scientific Films, Oxford Scientific Films; page 42 –
(left below) NASA, Science Photo Library, (below) Space
Telescope Science Institute, NASA, Science Photo Library;
page 43 – Sally Morgan, Ecoscene; page 44 – John Sandford,
Science Photo Library; page 45 – NOAO, Science Photo
Library

Contents

Introduction

Our eyes give us one of the most important senses, that of sight. They are not only sensitive to changes in brightness but also to the different colours in the light that reaches them. If our eyes could only sense brightness, we would see in 'black and white', like an old television programme, or film. Colour gives us valuable extra information which helps us to understand the world in which we live.

The use of colour is very important in science. It helps scientists to understand what they are seeing.

In this book we will look at what colour is, how colours are formed, and how we see them. We will also look at some of the many uses which are made of colours in science.

Colour and light are closely related. You cannot understand one without knowledge of the other. So we are going to look first at how light is produced.

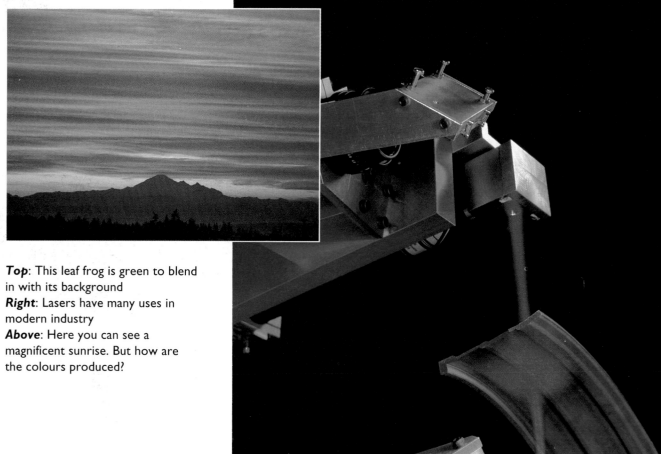

Top: This leaf frog is green to blend in with its background
Right: Lasers have many uses in modern industry
Above: Here you can see a magnificent sunrise. But how are the colours produced?

Top: These amazing patterns of colour have formed on the surface of oil

Left: This swallowtail butterfly looks very colourful. Look at the black and white one above and see how different it is

7

Light sources

The source of light that we know best is the sun. The sun is like a huge nuclear power station. It is made entirely of very hot gases. The heat and pressure from these gases make a continuous **nuclear reaction.** This **generates** lots of energy in the form of light.

The sun is a natural source of light. But light can be produced artificially from many different sources. The one that we know best is the light bulb. Do you know how a light bulb works?

A normal household light bulb is made up of a thin wire, called a **filament,** inside a glass bulb. The filament is attached to a base which is plugged into the electricity supply through a light socket. As the electricity passes through the filament, it has to fight its way along. In doing so, the electricity uses up some of its energy. This energy is given off as heat. The filament becomes white hot and glows. We see this as light.

The glass bulb around the filament has two uses. It protects the delicate filament and it also holds some gas. If a hot filament was exposed to air it would react, or change, as it met with the oxygen in the air, and it would slowly burn

Above: When electricity is passed along a filament of a light bulb it gets very hot and starts to glow
Right: Fluorescent lights use less electricity than light bulbs. This low energy fluorescent tube uses even less electricity

Top: Cities are lit up at night by thousands of light bulbs. These lights can even be seen from Space
Left: Fluorescent tubes last much longer than light bulbs. Here they are being tested to see how long they last
Below: Many street lights are sodium lamps that give out a yellow glow (see page 10)

away. To stop this happening, the bulb contains a small amount of a special **inert** gas which does not affect the filament. A gas called argon is used in most household light bulbs.

You may have heard of 'halogen' bulbs. Halogen bulbs are very popular because they give off a very bright white light. Bulbs which use a glowing filament are called incandescent lights.

Fluorescent lights work in a different way. They are glass tubes filled with mercury **vapour**, which is like a mist. Each end of the glass tube is connected to the electricity supply. When the electricity is switched on, the electrical current makes the tiny **molecules** in the vapour move around. As they move around they give off energy. The inside wall of the tube is coated with a **fluorescent** material which absorbs, or soaks up this energy and gives off a white light. Fluorescent tubes use less electricity to generate the same amount of light as an incandescent bulb. They also last longer, but they are more expensive to make.

You will have seen similar tubes, glowing in bright colours on shop signs and advertising. These are not fluorescent tubes; they are discharge tubes. The light is

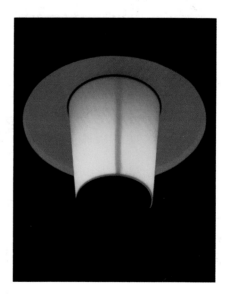

Right: The dazzling colours of fireworks are produced by different chemicals burning in the air

Above: The female glow-worm can produce her own eerie green light to signal or communicate with other glow-worms

COLOURFUL WORDS!

nuclear reaction: energy given out when a nucleus or the inside of a tiny atom, breaks down

generates: produces power

filament: a thin thread of metal

inert: not easily changed

vapour: a kind of mist, with tiny drops of liquid in the air

molecule: the smallest particle of a substance which can exist by itself

fluorescent: absorbing light of one colour and giving out light of another

current: a flow of electricity

produced by passing an electric **current** through a gas. Neon gas glows a bright red. Blue light is given off by tubes using a mixture of neon gas and mercury vapour.

Sodium lights are often used for street lighting. They always have a yellow glow. Sodium is a solid metal, but it reacts very dangerously with other substances such as oxygen and water, so it has to be sealed carefully in its glass tube. A large amount of electricity has to be passed through sodium to change it into a vapour, before it will give off light.

Fireworks are very colourful, and make light in yet another way. Their colours are produced by chemicals burning in the air. Different chemicals burn with a different colour.

Some animals, such as fireflies and glow-worms, give off light, and glow in the dark. This type of light is called 'bio-luminescence', and it is produced by chemical reactions inside the animal's body. Some plants and fungi are also bio-luminescent, such as the honey fungus.

Finally, light can be produced by **radioactive particles**. As a particle changes, or breaks up into a new form, a weak greenish light is given off as energy. Soldiers sometimes use lights like this for map-reading – they are called 'beta lights'. They do not need any batteries or other power sources to make them work. But once these lights stop glowing, they cannot be recharged.

This honey fungus looks normal in daylight but at night it can glow in the dark

COLOURFUL THINGS TO DO!

You can see for yourself how sodium produces a yellow light, by carrying out a simple experiment.

Clues from colours – a flame test
Do not do this experiment without an adult to help you.

You will need a piece of thick copper wire, 20cm long, a cork, some table salt and a gas flame.

1 Push one end of the wire into the cork. This is important because the wire will get hot and the cork will stop the heat reaching your fingers.

2 Dampen the end of the wire and dip it into some salt – the salt should stick to the end.

3 Light the gas and place the salty end of the wire into the flame.

What colour is the flame? Which chemical do you think might be in the salt? Check your answer by looking to see what is the main ingredient listed on the salt packet. You could try this with other chemicals in the kitchen, such as cream of tartar and Epsom salts. The colour of the flame depends on the chemical in the substance being tested. Scientists use the flame test to help them find out what certain substances are.

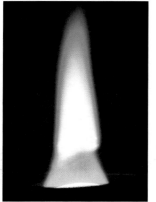

Copper burns with a green flame

COLOURFUL WORDS!

radioactive: a substance which breaks down by itself into smaller pieces, giving out energy as it breaks down

particles: very tiny pieces of a substance

11

Colour of light

We often say that light which comes from the sun or a light bulb looks white. We call it 'white light'.

However, white light is not a single colour but a mixture of lots of different colours, called a spectrum. You can see a spectrum when you look at a rainbow. There are seven colours in a spectrum. They are red, orange, yellow, green, blue, indigo and violet. The colours which we can see are known as the 'visible spectrum'.

Light is made of streams of particles called photons, or tiny packets of light. These travel in waves. The waves are just like ripples which spread outwards after a stone is thrown into a pond. Each colour of light is formed from waves of a different length. These wavelengths are very, very small – less than one millionth of a metre long.

White light can be split into a spectrum by using a specially shaped piece of glass called a prism. As the white light passes through the prism it is bent. But each colour

Light travels in waves like ripples on the surface of water

When a beam of white light is passed through a glass prism, the beam is bent and the seven colours that make up white light are separated. A spectrum is formed. How many colours can you see?

The wavelengths of light are very small. The wavelength of red light is slightly longer than that of blue light

will bend by a different amount, because each has a different wavelength. Red light will bend the most and blue the least. Bending light in this way is called refraction. Refraction causes the different colours of the spectrum to be separated. We can see each colour as it separates.

The experiment with the glass prism was first carried out by Sir Isaac Newton in 1666. He made a small hole in the blind across his window and allowed a beam of sunlight to pass through it. He then placed a prism in the path of the light so that when the light shone through the prism, the colours separated out into a spectrum. He then passed the spectrum through a second prism, which bent the coloured light back again into a beam of white light. With this

COLOURFUL THINGS TO DO!

Making a rainbow

You can easily produce your own rainbow on a sunny day. You will need a clear, round drinking glass, a piece of white paper and some water.

1 Fill the glass with water, right to the top.

2 Place the glass on a window ledge in full sunlight.

3 Place a piece of white paper on the floor in front of the window.

As the light passes through the glass, the colours are separated. If you move the paper around in the path of the light, you will find a place where a rainbow has been formed. Now you can see the visible spectrum.

experiment, Isaac Newton proved that white light is made of different colours. He published these discoveries in his book, *Opticks*, in 1704.

A rainbow is formed when raindrops in the air bend rays of light from the sun. The sunlight passes through the raindrops and is split into the seven colours, so we see a spectrum. Have you seen a spectrum anywhere else?

Sir Isaac Newton was the first scientist to prove that white light is made of many different colours

COLOURFUL THINGS TO DO!

Why does the sky look blue?

You will need a clear, rectangular plastic container, a torch, some powdered milk and a sheet of white card.

1 Fill the plastic container with water and place it on a table.
2 Place the light beam from a torch at one end so that the beam of light passes through the water.
3 Add a little powdered milk, a pinch at a time, so that you can see clearly the light beam passing through the water.
4 Look at the beam from the side and then from the end.
5 Now hold a white card at the end of the container.

The beam should look blue from the side, and orange from the end. If you have added enough powdered milk you should see the colour of the beam change from bluey-white to orangey-yellow along the length of the beam.

milk powder

clear plastic container filled with water

In the experiment, the white light from the torch shines through the water, just as the sun shines through the Earth's **atmosphere**. As it does so, the torchlight bumps into particles in the water, just as sunlight bumps into dust particles in the air. These particles make the light scatter. The shorter wavelengths get scattered more than the longer ones, so blue light is scattered the most. Yellow and red light can pass between the particles more easily, without bumping into them.

When the sun is setting, it is very low on the horizon, and light has to travel further through the air to get to your eyes. By the time the light reaches your eyes most of the blue light has been scattered, and only orange or red light is left to colour the sky. During the day, the sun is higher in the sky and light has less distance to travel to Earth. So less light is scattered and more blue light reaches your eyes.

Does this give you any idea why street lamps are often an orange colour? Well, in foggy weather, when there is a lot of water vapour in the air, the orange light from the street lamps is not scattered as much as blue would be. The orange light helps us to see better through the fog.

Top: Here you can see a beautiful sunset with the red sky reflected in the water of the lake
Above: A rainbow forms when sunlight passes through raindrops and is split up into the seven colours of the spectrum

COLOURFUL WORDS!

atmosphere: the layer of gases which surrounds the Earth

Invisible colour

You have seen how white light can be split into the visible spectrum, or the spectrum that can be seen. However, some wavelengths of light cannot be seen. They are outside our visible spectrum. Beyond the red end of the spectrum is Infra-red (or IR for short) and beyond the violet end is Ultra-violet (or UV). **Infra** means 'below' in the Latin language and **Ultra** means above, so you can see why these words are used.

Infra-red

If you have ever stood near a bonfire you will have felt heat **radiating** from the fire. This heat comes mainly from IR radiation.

IR radiation is given off by most things – it comes from molecules which are **vibrating** rapidly and giving off energy. As molecules get hotter, they vibrate more and the wavelength of the radiation gets shorter. When something is red hot, some of the wavelengths are so short that they are visible to the eye. So a red-hot fire gives off some of its energy as light, and some as heat or IR.

London looks very different when photographed using Infra-red film. The pale blue areas are buildings. The red areas show healthy vegetation such as woods

Flowers look very different when photographed using IR film. How many differences can you spot between the IR photo on the left and the one taken with a normal colour film?

Filament light bulbs give off 20 per cent of their energy as light, but the rest is given off as heat in the form of IR radiation. You have probably noticed that light bulbs become quite hot after they have been switched on for a while.

Although humans cannot see IR, other animals can. The common goldfish has eyes which can see IR. Some snakes have special **organs**, one on each side of the their head, which are sensitive to IR. They use these organs to find food by detecting the heat given off by the bodies of their **prey**. This allows the snake to find its prey at night, when the prey cannot see the snake!

People have made IR cameras to collect and focus IR rays just like an ordinary camera focuses visible light. The light falls on special photo film which can detect IR. When this film is developed, an IR picture is produced. This is called Infra-red false-colour, and it is often used by **satellites** when they are taking pictures of the Earth. The result is a sort of 'heat picture' of the Earth's surface. Such photos are very useful for weather forecasting, and for studying the Earth's vegetation.

Goldfish have eyes that can detect Infra-red, a colour that we cannot see

IR is also used by modern automatic cameras, to measure distance for focusing the picture, and for setting the strength of the flash. If you have ever used a remote control for a TV, Hi-fi or video, the chances

are that it also uses IR. In this case, IR is used to transmit, or send, signals from the remote control to the main equipment. Why do you think that IR is used rather than a visible wavelength of light?

Thermograms

A thermogram is a heat picture. It is taken with a special camera which detects Infra-red radiation. The colours of a thermogram show how much heat is being given out by the objects which the camera is filming. These coloured pictures have many uses. They are used in medical research, for finding diseased parts of the body. The diseased parts give off more heat than the healthy ones, and therefore show up as a different colour on the thermogram. Thermograms are also used by firemen, who locate living people in smoke-filled rooms by detecting the heat from their bodies. They can also show how much heat is lost from a house, and which parts lose the most, so that the owner knows where to put extra **insulation**.

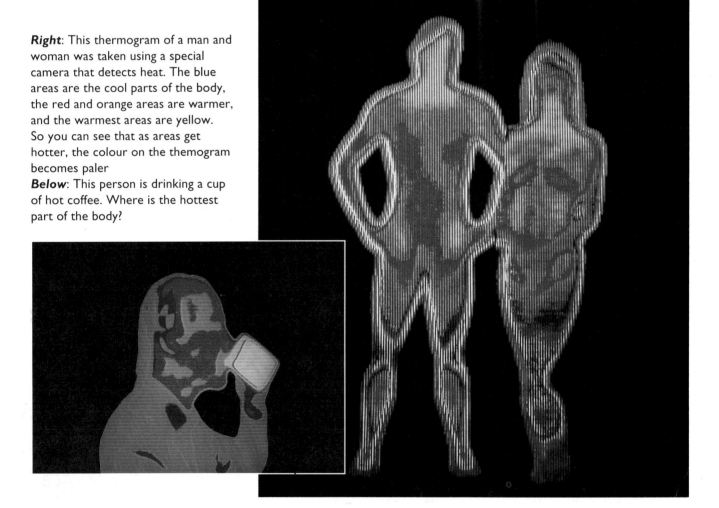

Right: This thermogram of a man and woman was taken using a special camera that detects heat. The blue areas are the cool parts of the body, the red and orange areas are warmer, and the warmest areas are yellow. So you can see that as areas get hotter, the colour on the themogram becomes paler
Below: This person is drinking a cup of hot coffee. Where is the hottest part of the body?

UV can damage our eyes. Arc welders have to wear a pair of protective dark green goggles to stop UV from damaging their eyes. An arc is a luminous beam of electricity

Ultra-violet

UV light, like IR, cannot be seen but there is a lot of UV in sunlight. It gives sunbathers' skin a tan, but too much UV can damage the skin. You may know someone who has been sunburnt by staying out in the sun too long. Human skin protects itself from the sun by making a brown pigment called melanin. It is the melanin which gives a person a tan. Dark-skinned people from sunny areas of the world are born with a lot of this pigment in their skin to give them protection. But people with fairer skin from the cooler parts of the world do not have so much, and can burn more easily. Too much exposure to sun can even cause skin **cancers**. These mainly affect people with fairer skin who spend a lot of time in the sun, and is a particular problem in countries such as Australia.

But our bodies do need some UV to stay healthy. UV is used by cells in the skin to make **vitamin D**. People who do not get much exposure to sunlight often develop diseases such as rickets. Someone with this disease has bones which soften and bend. This can be cured by eating foods with a lot of vitamin D in them, or by taking vitamin pills. In bad cases, UV lamps are used to give the patient an artificial dose of UV.

Have you ever seen glasses which are normally clear, but which go dark automatically in sunlight? They are quite popular. The glass contains crystals of a substance called silver halide, which turns dark in UV light. As the sunlight gets stronger, it contains more UV, and so the sunglasses go darker. They take only a few seconds to change colour.

Some chemicals glow when they absorb UV light. This effect is called fluorescence, and it is the secret of 'whiter than white' washing powders. The chemicals from which these washing powders are made absorb the UV in sunlight and glow slightly, making your clothes look much brighter than normal. If you go to a disco where there is a UV light, you will probably see white clothes glowing brightly in the dark. This is because they were washed in one of these powders that can absorb artificial UV light.

UV can be detected by many insects. Flowers often have petals with markings on them which reflect UV. We cannot see these markings, but bees can see them very clearly. They guide the bees more easily to the nectar in the middle of the flower.

Ozone is a special form of oxygen. It is a natural **filter** for UV radiation, and it occurs in a layer found high up in the atmosphere. This layer of ozone absorbs some of the harmful UV in sunlight.

The evening primrose has a yellow flower but when seen under UV light the black guidelines are clearly visible

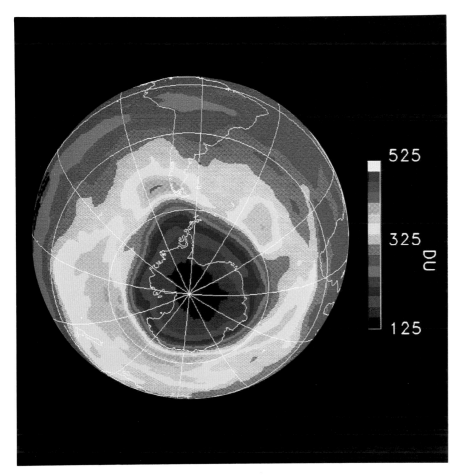

525

325 DU

125

We cannot see the ozone hole, but scientists can use special instruments to measure the ozone layer. The pink, purple and black areas over the Antarctic show where the ozone layer is thinnest

You may have heard of the 'ozone hole'. This is an area over the Antarctic which has lost much of its ozone because of chemical damage caused by **pollutants**. Over the years, Chloro-Fluorocarbons (or CFCs), have been released from fridges and aerosol sprays, and have slowly built up in the upper atmosphere where they break down the ozone. It is a very slow process, and we know that still more damage will be done by chemicals that were released during the 1980s. If the ozone layer is destroyed, then more UV will reach the surface of the Earth, and skin cancers and eye damage will become far more common.

Invisible Ink

Fluorescence in UV light can be used as a type of invisible ink. This is often used as a method of security marking. Postcodes are written on valuable goods using a special UV ink. The postcode is invisible under normal light, so a thief will not be able to cover it up. But it can be read under UV light because it makes the ink glow. If stolen goods are found by the police, and they have been invisibly marked, they can be scanned by UV light and returned to their owners.

COLOURFUL WORDS!

radiating: when rays and particles are given off by an object

vibrating: moving or quivering very quickly up and down or backwards and forwards

organ: a part of the body which has a particular job to do

pollutant: a harmful substance

prey: an animal killed by another animal for food

satellites: machines which are sent up into Space to revolve around the Earth

insulation: something which stops heat from escaping

cancer: a disease which eats away the body

vitamins: substances found in small amounts in food; they keep the body healthy

filter: a sieve which traps all particles bigger than a certain size, and which lets through smaller ones

pollutant: a harmful substance, which often poisons other things

Colour perception

We use filters every day. Suntan lotions contain filters that block UV light. This stops our skin from getting burnt in the sun

Glass can be made in many different colours. How many colours can you see in this picture?

What we see as colour is called colour perception. It is important to understand that the colour of any object that we see comes from the colour of the light which bounces back, or is reflected from it. So, if you shine a white light onto a piece of cloth which absorbs all colours of light except red, then the cloth appears red. The red light which is left from the white light bounces back and gets scattered.

What would happen if you shone a blue light onto the red cloth? The cloth would absorb all of the blue light and there would be no red light in it to scatter, so the dress would look black. No red light would be reflected from the cloth. You could test this for yourself using a torch and some coloured filters.

Filtering light

Filters are made to allow certain things to pass through. For example, a sieve is used to filter out large objects and let the smaller particles through. In the same way, we can use

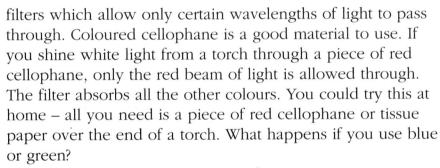

This field of poppies looks very different when it is viewed through a red filter (top) and a blue filter (above). How many differences can you see?

filters which allow only certain wavelengths of light to pass through. Coloured cellophane is a good material to use. If you shine white light from a torch through a piece of red cellophane, only the red beam of light is allowed through. The filter absorbs all the other colours. You could try this at home – all you need is a piece of red cellophane or tissue paper over the end of a torch. What happens if you use blue or green?

Filters are very important in our lives. We use suncreams to filter out the harmful UV in sunlight, and so stop our skin from burning when we lie in the sun. Some animals have natural filters in their skin. Many tree frogs which look green, actually have blue bodies. But blue would make them very visible to their **predators**, so they **camouflage** themselves with a transparent yellow skin. The yellow skin acts as a filter, allowing only yellow light through. Then the yellow joins with the blue colour of the frog's skin to allow only green light to be reflected.

There are many man-made filters in use today. Most of them are made from glass. The different coloured filters are made by adding special substances to the **raw materials** of glass, which are limestone, soda and sand. The metal, chromium, for example, gives glass a yellow appearance, while another metal, cobalt, makes it blue. These filters are used in photography to correct colours, or to achieve special effects.

COLOURFUL WORDS!

predators: animals which feed on other animals

camouflage: to hide by using colour and shape

raw material: the basic materials from which other things are made

Mixing light

Mixing coloured light is not the same as mixing coloured paint. There are three primary colours of light which can make all the other colours when they are mixed. These are not the same as the primary colours in your paintbox. They are red, green and blue. If you mix all three primary colours together, you get white.

When green and red light are mixed, they make yellow. When red and blue light are mixed, they make a colour called magenta. Blue and green light together make a colour called cyan. These colours – yellow, magenta and cyan are called secondary colours. Mixing light in this way is called colour addition.

However, we see most things by reflected light. The objects we see get their colour by what is called colour subtraction, or taking away certain colours. An object absorbs certain wavelengths of light which fall on it, and reflects the rest. The reflected wavelengths give the object its colour. If white light falls on an object which absorbs red and green wavelengths, the object will appear blue. The leaves of plants look green because leaves absorb the red and blue light and reflect the green.

Leaves look green because they absorb red and blue light and reflect green. It is the reflected green light which we can see

The primary colours of red, blue and green will produce white if they are all mixed together. When two primary colours are mixed, a secondary colour is formed. What are the three secondary colours?

24

Mixing light to make hidden shapes and words

If you look at the shape below through a red filter or piece of red cellophane, some of the coloured lines will disappear, while others will turn black. A new shape will appear. What shape can you see? The red filter lets only red light pass through. The light reflected from the green and blue lines is blocked by the filter, so these lines look black.

You can do this yourself. You could copy the same shape but using different colours, you could try to make your own shape. Remember that red, orange, pink and yellow will seem to disappear when you look through the red filter. But colours such as blue, green and purple will appear to be black.

Now write your name with coloured felt-tip pens on a piece of white paper, using a different coloured pen for each letter. When you look at your name through the red filter some of the letters disappear. Try to write a letter that contains a hidden message to a friend. Your friend will have to use a red filter as a decoder, to read the hidden message.

You will need many different coloured crayons to write a hidden message to your friend. Make sure you have blue, green, red, orange, pink and yellow

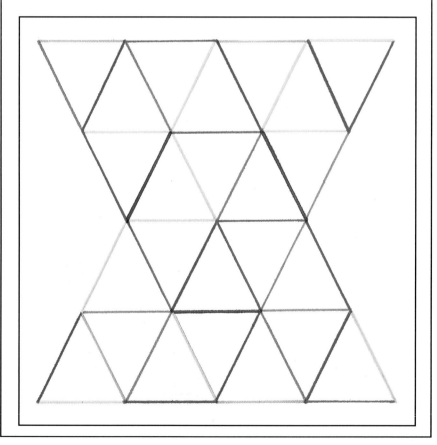

COLOURFUL THINGS TO DO!

Mixing light and making coloured shadows

You will need three torches, one covered with red cellophane, one with blue and the last with green. You will also need a white wall, and a friend to help you. Make sure the room is dark before you start.

1 Shine the torches onto the white wall, overlapping the coloured beams of light. What colours can you produce when you do this? You will also see from this experiment that shadows are not always black – the colour of the shadow depends on the colour of the light which falls on the object.

2 Using the filtered torches, ask your friend to hold a hand in front of the point where there is white light. This is where the three beams overlap.

3 Move around the position of the torches so that you can see three different coloured shadows.

4 Turn off one of the torches so that light from just two overlaps. What happens to the colour of the shadows now? Try this experiment using the other **combinations** of colours. Does the colour of the shadows change if your friend puts a coloured object in front of the wall instead of a hand?

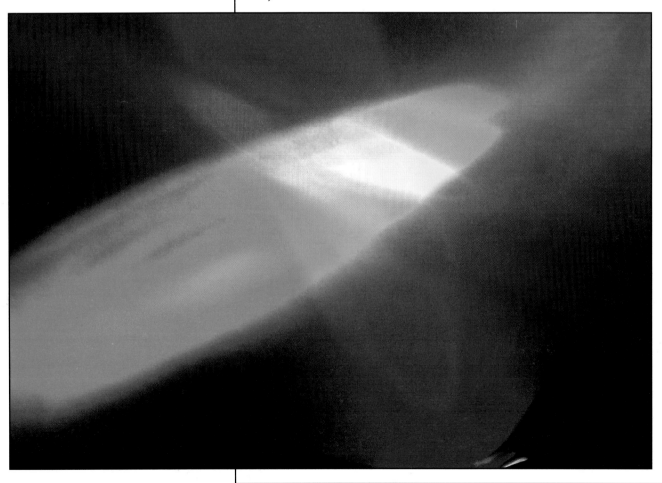

COLOURFUL THINGS TO DO!

Spinning discs

You can prove that white light is made from a mixture of all three primary colours together. You will need a circle of white card, some red, blue and green paint or felt-tipped pens, a sharp pencil and a protractor. You can use paint instead of felt pens if you wish.

1 Using the protractor, divide the disc into three equal sections as shown in the photograph.

2 Paint each section a different colour.

3 Make a hole in the middle of the disc and fit it over the pencil.

4 Spin the disc very fast on the point of the pencil. What colour can you see?

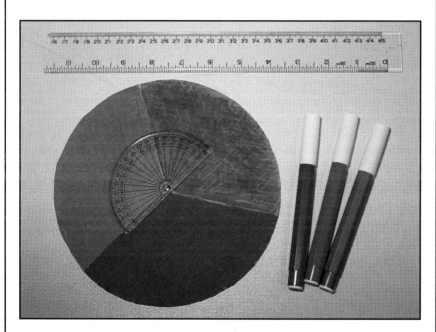

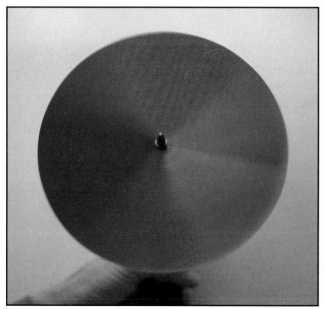

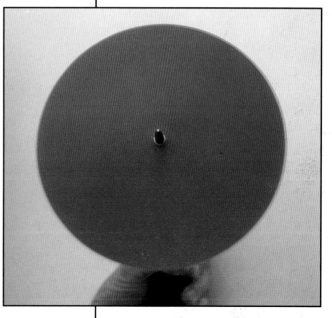

When the disc begins to spin the colours blur together. If it spins fast enough a white colour will be visible

27

Colour television

A colour television works by mixing the three primary light colours. It also fools the eye into seeing colours which are

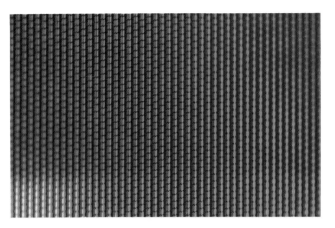

not really there at all. A TV screen is covered in thousands of tiny coloured dots called **pixels**. Pixels are laid out across the screen in long lines of the colours red, green, blue; red, green, blue and so on. Each tiny coloured dot can be made to glow. If three neighbouring pixels glow together, the eye sees white. If red and green only are lit, then yellow will be seen and so on.

The whole screen is **scanned** 50 times a second to build up a continuous moving picture. To give an even greater range of colours, and shades of one colour, the brightness of each pixel can be changed. In Europe, the TVs have 625 lines of pixels on the screen. Can you imagine how many times a pixel is lit while you watch a complete film? You can see the pixels on your own TV. Turn it on and look at a tiny part through a magnifying glass. Do not look at it for too long, though, as it could harm your eyes.

Colour printing works in a similar way. If you look at a colour photograph in this book with a magnifying glass, you will see the same pattern of coloured pixels. To produce a colour picture, four colours are needed; yellow, magenta, cyan and black. Almost any colour can be produced by using these four colours. A full-colour picture is made by first printing the yellow dots, then magenta, cyan and black.

If you look very carefully at a colour television screen you will see tiny dots of colour called pixels. There are rows of three colours – red, green and blue. By combining these three colours, all the other colours can be made. There is a patch of yellow at the bottom of the picture. This is because red and green pixels have been lit up to make yellow

Mixing colours for printing pigment is not as easy as mixing colours of light. That is why we need the secondary colours of yellow, magenta and cyan
Right: The coloured photographs in this book have been made using tiny dots of colour, just like those on a television screen
Far right: When a picture is magnified, it is possible to see the tiny dots of colour. Here you can see yellow, magenta, cyan and black

COLOURFUL THINGS TO DO!

Making colours

This experiment shows how black and white can be mixed to make us see colours. You will need a circle of white card, a pair of compasses, a black felt-tipped pen and a thin stick.

1 Carefully draw lines on the circle of card as shown in the diagram. Make sure the black lines are quite thin.

2 Make a hole in the middle, large enough to fit over the pencil.

3 Now make the card spin. It might be easier to ask an adult to make the card spin fast by using a hand or electric drill, an electric screwdriver, or even the turntable of a record player.

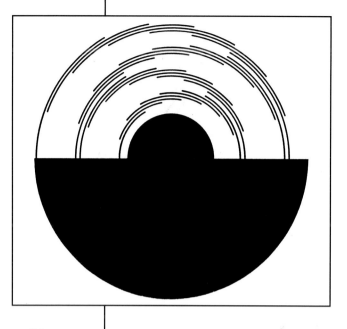

Can you see coloured circles? If you spin the disc in the other direction, you will see other colours. It is better to spin the disc in sunlight or under a normal light bulb, as it does not work so well in fluorescent light.

In what order do the coloured bands appear? What colour is in the centre? Is the order the same if you spin the disc in the opposite direction?

Scientists have great difficulty in explaining how this experiment works. But they think that it is because of the way the human eye responds to patterns, and how the brain understands the messages which the eye sends it. The brain is fooled into thinking that there is really some colour to be seen, because it is not used to getting this type of image from the eye.

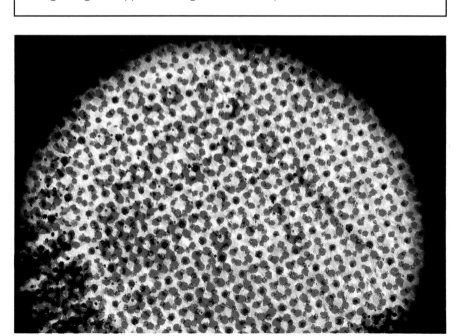

COLOURFUL WORDS!

combinations: things which are joined or are used together

pixel: a tiny dot, used to make up a picture

image: picture

scanned: when a beam is passed over every part of the screen

Interference patterns

The brilliant colours seen on soap bubbles, and when oil floats on water, are made by a process called interference. Light rays are reflected from both the inside and outside surfaces of the soap bubble. A light ray that is reflected from the inside has to travel further than a ray from the outside. When some of the rays meet, they are slightly out of step, so they interfere with each other. Some of the meeting rays cancel each other out, but others join to form bands of colour. Bands like these can also be seen on the surface of a compact disc when you tilt it into the light (see page 33).

The **iridescent** colours of a butterfly's wing are also produced by interference. A butterfly's wings are covered in tiny scales. Each scale has thousands of tiny ridges and grooves on its surface. These cause the light to be reflected in interference patterns, forming beautiful bands of colour.

COLOURFUL WORDS!

iridescent: shiny rainbow-like colours

The wings of a butterfly are covered in tiny scales that reflect light. This gives the butterfly's wing a lovely, shimmering appearance

Giant bubbles

You will need a large flat container, two large tablespoonfuls of washing-up liquid, a tablespoonful of glycerine (or sugar), a wire coat-hanger and some wool.

1 Fill the container with water.

2 Add the washing-up liquid and the glycerine and mix well. The mixture works best if it is left overnight before it is used.

3 Make a round hoop out of the coat-hanger, leaving a length as a handle.

4 Wrap the wool around the wire hoop.

5 Hold the hoop, pass it through the water and lift it out vertically. You should now have a film of water on your hoop which has many bands of colour.

6 Now sweep the loop gently through the air to form a huge bubble, and twist the hoop to release it.

You could try this again, making the wire coat-hanger into other shapes, or even into interlocking loops, so that they make a figure-of-eight.

If you look carefully at soap bubbles you will see brilliant bands of colour caused by interference. If you change the position of your head, the bands of colour disappear

Lasers

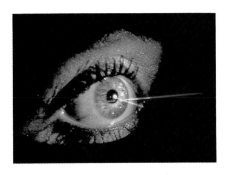

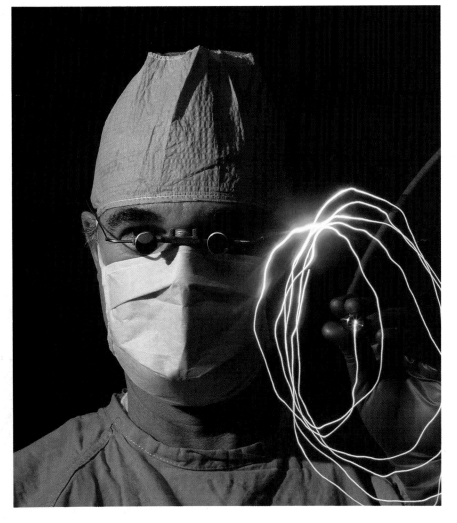

The word 'laser' comes from the capital letters of '**L**ight **A**mplification by **S**timulated **E**mission of **R**adiation', which describes how laser light is produced.

Lasers have a number of features which are very important to scientists. They produce a narrow beam of light which can travel for long distances without spreading out. All the photons, or little packets of light, 'line up' with one another exactly. We say that they are 'in phase', or 'coherent'. Also, laser light is very 'pure', as it is made from light of only one wavelength.

Lasers can be made from a tube containing a mixture of gases such as helium and neon. The tube has a mirror at each end. Electricity is used to excite the gas, or make the molecules in it move around. This causes the gas to flash. The light waves are bounced backwards and forwards by

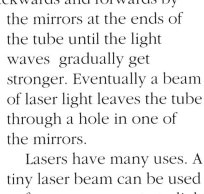

the mirrors at the ends of the tube until the light waves gradually get stronger. Eventually a beam of laser light leaves the tube through a hole in one of the mirrors.

Lasers have many uses. A tiny laser beam can be used to focus, or concentrate light energy into one small spot. Because of this, lasers are often used to cut through metals and other materials, or to read bar-codes on goods in shops and warehouses. Doctors sometimes use them in the treatment of disease, to cut away diseased **tissue,** or to unblock blood vessels. They can also be used to send telephone calls over very long distances, such as across the Atlantic Ocean, through special cables.

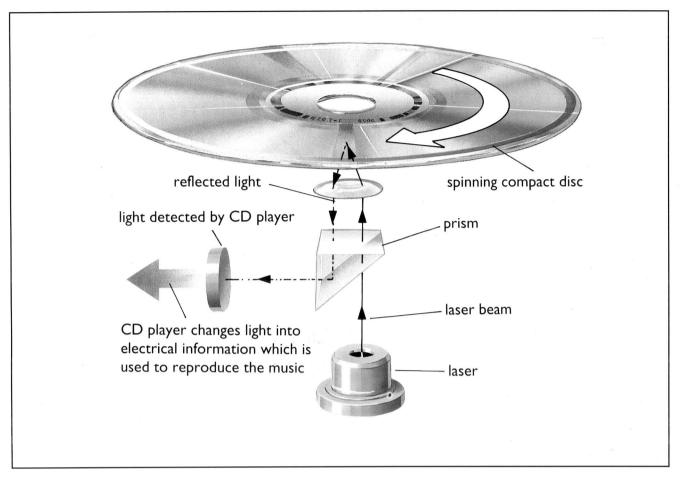

reflected light

light detected by CD player

spinning compact disc

prism

CD player changes light into electrical information which is used to reproduce the music

laser beam

laser

Lasers can even be used for entertainment, as special effects for rock concerts and light shows. Laser light-shows use carefully positioned mirrors to reflect the light over the heads of the audience. By moving the mirrors, the beams of light bounce off in special patterns.

Lasers are used to record and play back very large amounts of information on compact discs (CDs). This is because the beams of light can be made so narrow, and the wavelength of the light is so small. For example, a 12cm **diameter** CD can hold about 600 million **bytes** of information.

The shiny surface of the CD is covered in **microscopic** pits, or dents. As the disc spins, the laser lights up the pattern of pits. When the laser beam hits a pit its light is scattered. But if it hits the shiny surface, the beam of light is reflected and this is detected by the CD player. The CD player reads the track very quickly, giving a stream of information which is used to reproduce the music. With a record player, the grooves of a record are read by a needle, and both the needle and the record can wear out. But CDs do not wear out because there is no contact between the disc and the laser head.

Lasers are used to read the information contained on a compact disc

Laser light shone into one end of these optical fibres will not escape until it reaches the other end. Optical fibres are used to carry messages over long distances and to allow doctors to see inside a patient's body

Above: Holograms are found on bank cards and credit cards. They make it difficult to produce forgeries of the card
Left: A hologram of a whole champagne glass combines with the real lower half of a broken one
Below: Many supermarket checkouts have bar-code readers that scan the bar-code on an item and allow the price to be entered automatically into the till. This makes adding up the cost of the goods much quicker

COLOURFUL WORDS!

tissue: material

diameter: the width of a circle, measuring through the point in the centre

bytes: pieces of information, like the letters of the alphabet

microscopic: too small to be seen by the eye; a microscope is needed

three-dimensional: not flat – having the appearance of depth

forge: to copy something that you are not allowed to copy

An experiment by NASA, the North American Space Authority, shows just how far laser light can travel. Astronauts who landed on the moon in 1969 left behind mirrors. These were used to reflect laser beams back to Earth, so that scientists could measure the distance between the Earth and the moon very accurately indeed.

Holograms are made using lasers. Holograms are **three-dimensional** pictures which change their appearance as you look at them from different angles. You may have seen holograms in novelty shops, but they are also used on credit cards, because they are very difficult to **forge**.

COLOURFUL THINGS TO DO!

Make a kaleidoscope

Not everybody has the chance to see a laser working, but you could try to see how light bounces by making a kaleidoscope. You should have an adult with you when you do this, as glass can be very dangerous and the kaleidoscope will be heavy.

You will need six mirror tiles, or six plastic mirrors (30cm square), some sticky tape, and three pieces of strong cardboard each measuring 36cm x 60cm. You can use other shapes and sizes, too.

1 Place the six tiles in a row and tape them together. At every other join, leave enough room for the tape to bend and act as a hinge.

2 Fold up the bottom 6cm of each piece of cardboard to form a lip.

3 Tape the card together to form a large triangle, with the lip on the inside.

4 Form the tiles into a triangle and insert them into the cardboard triangle (see top picture).

You now have a kaleidoscope. Ask somebody to hold it while you duck under and put your head inside (see bottom picture). You should see lots of faces (all your own!). These are reflections of reflections. The artist has shown only three reflections. How many can you actually see?

Below: A pattern inside a real kaleidoscope

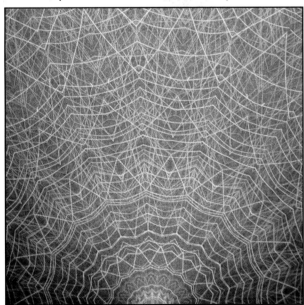

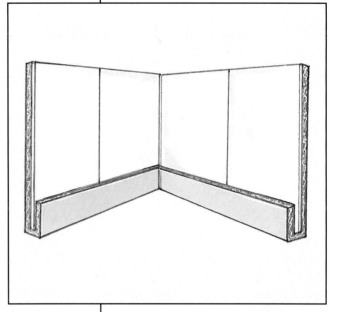

Polarized light

Sometimes light is reflected off the surface of water, making it difficult to see anything because of the glare. You may know that if you wear polarizing sunglasses, you can see below the water more clearly. This is because these glasses stop the glare. They in fact remove polarized light. How is this possible?

Light from the sun consists of light waves that vibrate in all directions. When light is reflected from flat surfaces, such as water, it becomes 'polarized'. This means that the reflected light is vibrating only in one direction, making it clearer and stronger. It gives a dazzling glare. The light coming from below the surface is still vibrating in all directions, because it has not been polarized.

Polarizing sunglasses use special filters to remove the light which is vibrating in one direction only. This takes away all of the reflected light from the surface of the water, but only some of the light from below the surface, so you can see what is at the bottom of the water more clearly. There is no glare, either. However, in order to do this, the filters in the sunglasses need to be at a certain angle.

One of these photographs of the Statue of Liberty was taken using a polarizing filter. This gives a photograph deeper colours. Which one was taken with the filter?

Take a pair of polarizing sunglasses, and on a bright day look at some water on a lake, pond or swimming pool. First, look at the water without the sunglasses, and then put them on. Can you see a difference? What position do the sunglasses have to be in to cut down the glare? The brightness of the sky will also change as you move around the polarizing glasses. Why do you think fishermen want to wear polarizing sunglasses on a sunny day?

Polarized light can have its uses. Some engineers use it to check whether something is damaged, or is about to break. For example, polarized light can be used to detect weaknesses in plastics. If it is shone onto the plastic, any weakness will cause the rays of light to interfere with one another. The light scatters or splits up and produces coloured light bands which, as we have seen before, are known as interference patterns. These patterns appear on the weak plastic. If the plastic has no weakness, then no patterns will be seen.

COLOURFUL THINGS TO DO!

Interference patterns

You will need two polarizing filters and a clear plastic ruler or protractor. You could use the lenses from an old pair of sunglasses, or perhaps get hold of a photographer's polarizing filters which are used on camera lenses.

1 Place the ruler between the two filters.

2 Now look at a light bulb through the ruler and the two filters. You should see some coloured bands.

3 If you bend the ruler slightly, the bands should move. The bands show the weaknesses in the plastic.

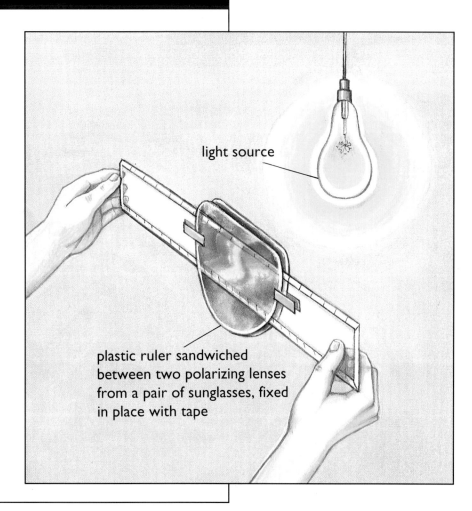

light source

plastic ruler sandwiched between two polarizing lenses from a pair of sunglasses, fixed in place with tape

Colour vision

Many animals can see colour. All birds and some mammals have this ability. How do our eyes see? Each eye is spherical, rather like a ping-pong ball. There is fluid inside to make sure that the eye keeps its shape and does not cave in. Our eye works just like a camera. The light enters at the front, through a thin transparent film called the cornea. It then passes through a lens and is brought to a sharp point, or focus, at the back of the eye. In a camera, the image is recorded on a film which is sensitive to light. The eye has a light-sensitive layer of cells instead, called the retina. The light is changed into electrical messages which are sent to the brain.

The cells of the retina allow us to see both in black and white, and in colour. There are two types of cell in the retina: rod and cone. There are about 125 million rods and they are far more sensitive to light than the cones. Each rod contains a small amount

Below: The black pupil can be seen easily in the eye of this cat
Bottom: This is a section through the eye of a human being

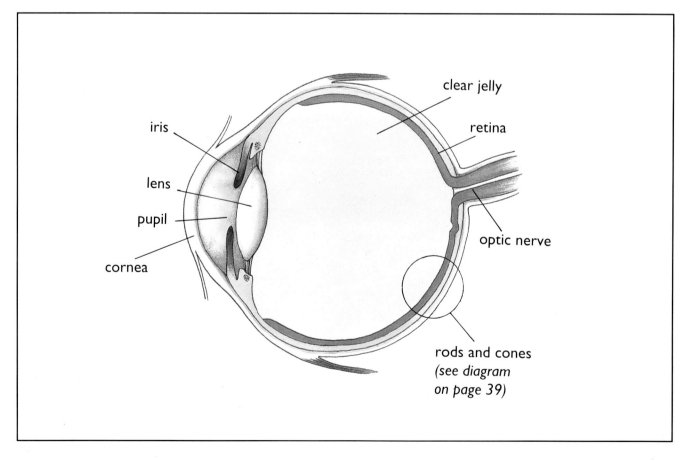

clear jelly

retina

iris

lens

pupil

cornea

optic nerve

rods and cones
(see diagram on page 39)

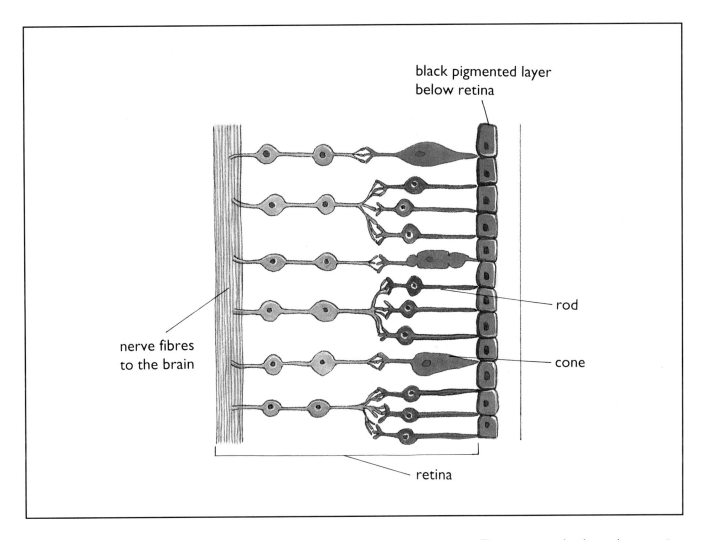

black pigmented layer
below retina

nerve fibres
to the brain

rod

cone

retina

of a light-sensitive chemical. When light falls on the chemical it produces a tiny electrical signal which is sent to the brain. Rods give us black-and-white vision and enable us to see in dim light. If you go out at night you will see only in black and white; you have no colour vision. This is because only the rods can work in these dim conditions. However, if you return to a brightly lit room, you can see in colour again.

Cones give us colour vision, but they need strong light before they will work. There are three types of cone – one for detecting blue light, one for red light and one for green. So how can you see all the different colours? It is rather like the way that spots of colours are mixed to produce a TV picture. Strong signals from a red cone and weak signals from nearby blue and green cones tell the brain that the colour being detected is red. If three neighbouring colour cones all send strong signals, the brain will recognize this as a spot of white light, and so on. The brain forms a picture from the many millions of different coloured spots of light.

The retina is a thin layer that contains thousands of rods and cones

COLOURFUL THINGS TO DO!

Bird in a cage

In this experiment, if you stare at a colour you will see it change. You will need four squares of white paper and four felt-tip pens – red, blue, green and black.

1 Draw the shape of a bird on three of the pieces of white paper. Make sure that the birds are all the same size.

2 Colour them in so that you have a red one, a blue one and a green one.

3 Draw a black eye on each bird.

4 Draw the shape of a bird-cage on the fourth white sheet, using the black pen. Make sure that the cage is large enough to cover the birds.

5 Make sure that you are in a brightly lit place. Take the sheet with the red bird and place it next to the bird-cage.

6 Stare at the eye of the red bird for 15 to 20 seconds, then quickly stare at the cage. You should see a blue/green (cyan) bird in the cage.

7 Repeat this with the blue bird. You should see a yellow bird in the cage.

What colour is the bird that appears in the cage when you look at the green bird?

You could try this with other shapes. How could you produce a blue banana in the cage?

In the experiment above the ghostly birds that appear in the cage are called after-images. An after-image is an image that stays with you even after you have stopped looking at something. But why does the colour change? When you stare at the red bird, the cones which are excited by red light get tired and stop working.

When you look at the cage your eyes can only respond to blue and green light, which mix to form the secondary colour, cyan. So, instead of a red bird you see a cyan bird.

COLOURFUL THINGS TO DO!

Colour contrasts

Some colours seem to change if you put them against different backgrounds. In this experiment you will look at certain colours on different coloured backgrounds. You will need an A3-sized piece of stiff card in any colour, and four A4-sized sheets of paper – two coloured the same blue, and two, the same orange. You will also need scissors and some glue.

1 Take the large piece of card and cover one half of it with orange paper, and the other half with blue paper.

2 Glue the paper in place.

3 Cut a small 10 cm square of orange and blue from the spare sheets of paper and place them on the background sheet, placing the blue square on the orange background, and the orange square on the blue background.

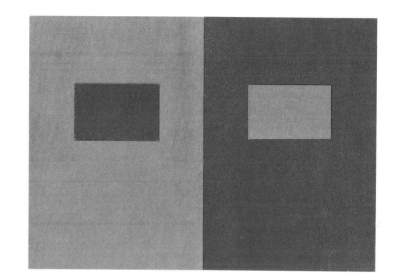

Look at the blue square on the orange background for a while. Then look at the blue background. You should notice that the colour of the blue square on the orange background looks a slightly different shade of blue when you compare it with the blue background. Why does this happen, even though you know that you cut the squares from the same coloured sheet? Does the same happen for the orange square?

You could try this with pieces of paper of other colours – yellow, purple, different shades of blue and orange, etc. Place squares of coloured paper of the same size and colour onto the orange and blue backgrounds. Can you see any differences in the colours of the squares or their backgrounds?

Above, the shades of colour change because your cones are fooling you. Orange is made up mainly of blue. We say that blue and orange are **complementary colours**. When cones in one part of your eye see blue light for a long time, they get tired and make nearby cones less sensitive to blue, so that when you look at the blue of the background, it looks less blue than it really is. This does not work with all combinations of colours. For example, yellow and blue are not complementary colours. So if you stare at a yellow square on a blue background, and then at a yellow background, the yellow will always look the same because it is made from red and green, not blue. So the red and green cones do not get so tired.

Early **astronomers** had similar experiences. When they looked at the planet Mars they saw a wave of green spreading down from the planet's North Pole as the volcanic Polar Cap disappeared from view each spring. However, we know now that the green is really a wave of grey volcanic dust. The planet has a red background, and grey on red actually looks green to human eyes.

Right below: In order to get a true colour picture of Mars, the same photograph was taken several times using red, green and blue filters. The red surface of Mars is easy to see when the photographs are combined
Below: There are several volcanoes on Mars and the one shown is Olympus Mons. Every springtime a wave of grey volcanic dust moves across the planet

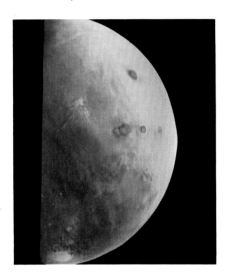

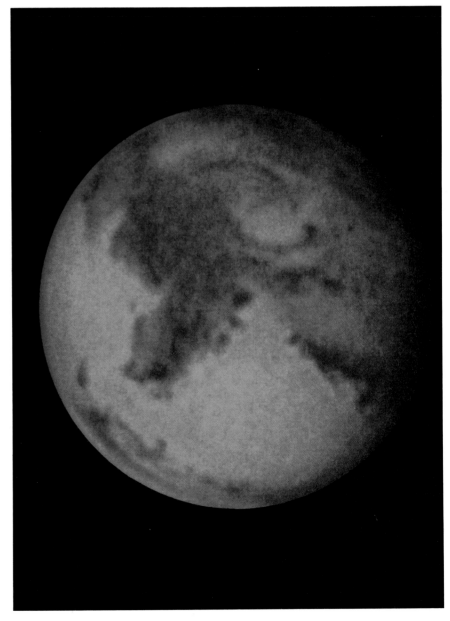

COLOURFUL WORDS!

astronomers: scientists who study Space – the planets, stars and so on

complementary colours: colours that are related to each other

Colour-blindness

When somebody cannot see colour properly, they are said to be 'colour-blind'. True colour-blindness is when you cannot see any colour at all. Anyone suffering from this would only be able to see in black, white and shades of grey. Fortunately, this is quite rare, and only one person in every 40,000 suffers from true colour-blindness. However, it is more common for people to be unable to see just one or two colours. For example, some people cannot tell the difference properly between red and green. Red and green colour-blindness affects more men than women. In Europe about one man in twelve will have some form of colour-blindness, but only one woman in 200 will suffer. You do not become colour-blind; you are born with colour-blindness. It usually gets passed down from parents to their children. We say it is inherited.

A colour-blind person leads a normal life. They can often guess the colour of something from its shade or position. However, it can be quite dangerous sometimes, such as in a factory where lights are usually coloured red for danger and green for safety. There is a simple set of tests which can be performed by a doctor to see if someone is colour-blind.

Left: The number 29 is clearly visible to somebody with normal colour vision, but a colour-blind person would not see it

Below: What would a person with red-green colour-blindness see?

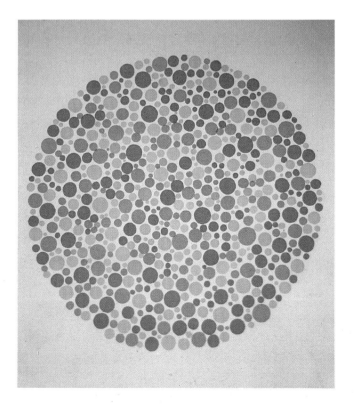

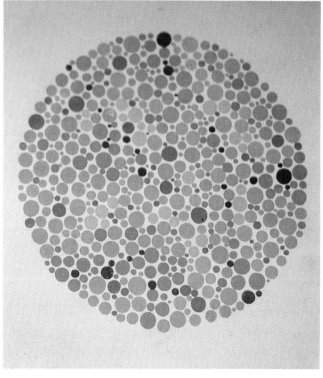

Learning from light

Because they are so far away, the light from stars may take many years to reach the Earth, even though light travels 300,000 km every second. The Earth is 150 million km from our own sun, and the light from the sun takes 8.5 minutes to travel this distance. Light from the next nearest star, which is called Proxima Centauri, takes over four years to reach us. We say that it is four **light years** away.

When you look at the North Star, you are looking at light that has taken 700 years to arrive, so you can see the star as it was 700 years ago. Light which is reaching us now from the furthest **galaxies** is almost as old as the **universe** itself. We may never be able to travel to the furthest stars, but by studying the light from them, scientists can discover from what materials they are made, and how they were formed.

The different colours of stars show their differences in temperature. The white stars are the hottest, while the orange-red ones are the coolest. The star called Spica in the Virgo **constellation** is a white star with a surface temperature of about 25,000°C. Sirius is a blueish-white star with a temperature of 11,000°C. Our sun is a yellow star with a cooler temperature of 6,000°C. Betelgeuse, in the constellation of Orion, is an orange-red super-giant with a temperature of 3,000°C. If you look at the stars through a telescope, you can see their colours and so work out how hot they are. Try this yourself at night, with a telescope or a good pair of binoculars. Never look at the sun through binoculars or a telescope, as you can damage your eyes very badly.

Light from a star is very weak by the time it reaches Earth, but it can be collected by a telescope and fed to an instrument called a spectroscope. This instrument acts like a prism and splits the light into a spectrum. The hot surface of a star gives out light of all wavelengths, but as the light leaves the star it passes through the star's own outer atmosphere of cool gases. The **elements** in this outer layer absorb certain wavelengths of light, so when we look at the star's

Orion is one of the most easily seen constellations in the sky. The bright pink-white star at the top is Betelgeuse – a red super-giant with a temperature of 3,000°C

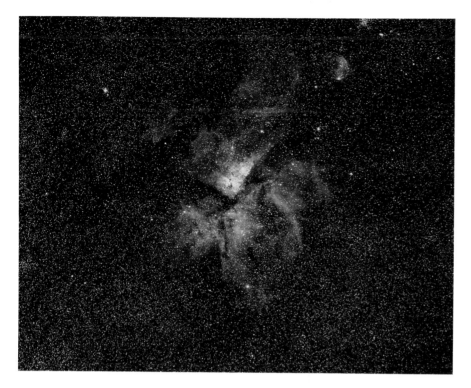

Left: The pink clouds of the Eta Carinae nebula tell us that it contains hydrogen gas
Above: The pink clouds of the Trifid nebula indicate hydrogen gas. However, the blue of the nebula to the top of the picture is only starlight

spectrum we see dark lines where light has been absorbed. From the position of these lines, scientists can work out which elements are present in the layer of cool gases. Scientists have now identified, or found, over 70 different elements in our sun. The element Helium was identified on the sun 25 years before it was found in the Earth's atmosphere. It was named after the Greek word for sun, helios.

A star's movement can also be studied using colour, by measuring something called Doppler shift. If you have ever stood at the side of a road as a car with its horn on passes you, you will probably have noticed that the tone goes up as it comes towards you, and down as it goes away. The sound waves have been moved, or 'Doppler shifted'. Light waves behave in the same way as sound waves, so when a star is moving away from us, the lines in its spectrum are shifted towards the red end. The amount of shift towards the red end can be measured, and it tells us how fast the star is moving.

Space itself is not as empty as it might seem. The light that we see in the night sky may have travelled through clouds of gas deep in Space. Each gas cloud is called a nebula and can be enormous. The gases that make up each cloud absorb light from the stars, so we can tell which gases are in the nebula by its colour. Pink nebulae (more than one nebula) contain hydrogen gas. Nebulae which contain oxygen and nitrogen appear to be blue-green.

COLOURFUL WORDS!

light year: the distance which light travels in one year

galaxies: systems, or large groups of stars, such as the Milky Way

universe: all the known galaxies

constellation: a cluster, or small group of stars; they make shapes and patterns in the sky and are given names such as the Plough, Orion, and so on

element: a substance that cannot be split chemically into a simpler substance, such as oxygen

Index

Books to read

How Science Works Judith Hann (Eyewitness Guide, DK)
Colour and Light, Fun with Science Series Barbara Taylor (Kingfisher)
Lights and Lasers Kathryn Whyman (Franklin Watts)
Exploring Light Ed Catherall (Wayland)